The Natural World
EUROPE

Megan Cuthbert

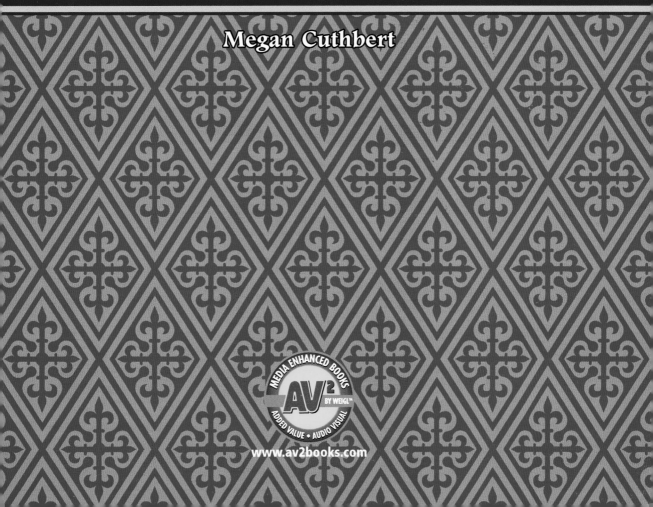

MEDIA ENHANCED BOOKS
AV2
BY WEIGL™
ADDED VALUE • AUDIO VISUAL

www.av2books.com

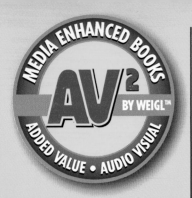

AV² provides enriched content that supplements and complements this book Weigl's AV² books strive to create inspired learning and engage young mind in a total learning experience.

Your AV² Media Enhanced books come alive with...

Audio
Listen to sections of the book read aloud.

Key Words
Study vocabulary, and complete a matching word activity.

Go to **www.av2books.com,** and enter this book's unique code.

Video
Watch informative video clips.

Quizzes
Test your knowledge.

BOOK CODE

K 3 2 7 6

Embedded Weblinks
Gain additional information for research.

Slide Show
View images and captions, and prepare a presentation.

AV² by Weigl brings you media enhanced books that support active learning.

Try This!
Complete activities and hands-on experiments.

... and much, much more

Published by AV² by Weigl
350 5th Avenue, 59th Floor
New York, NY 10118
Website: www.av2books.com   www.weigl.com

Library of Congress Cataloging-in-Publication Data

Cuthbert, Megan, author.
 Europe / Megan Cuthbert.
    pages cm. -- (The natural world)
Includes index.
 ISBN 978-1-4896-0950-2 (hardcover : alk. paper) -- ISBN 978-1-4896-0951-9 (softcover : alk. paper) --
ISBN 978-1-4896-0952-6 (single user ebk.) -- ISBN 978-1-4896-0953-3 (multi user ebk.)
1. Natural history--Europe--Juvenile literature. 2. Ecology--Europe--Juvenile literature. 3. Europe--Environmental conditions--Juvenile literature. I. Title.
 QH135.C88 2015
 578.094--dc23
                            2014004673

Printed in the United States of America in North Mankato, Minnesota
1 2 3 4 5 6 7 8 9 0 18 17 16 15 14

042014
WEP150314

Editor: Heather Kissock
Design: Mandy Christiansen

Every reasonable effort has been made to trace ownership and to obtain permission to reprint copyright material. The publishers would be pleased to have any errors or omissions brought to their attention so that they may be corrected in subsequent printings.

Weigl acknowledges Getty Images as its primary image supplier for this title.

Contents

Welcome to Europe!

Europe is the second smallest continent in the world. It covers approximately 4 million square miles (10 million sq. km). Even though Europe is relatively small, it has the third largest population of all the continents. Almost 740,000,000 people live throughout more than 45 countries.

The European landscape varies greatly. It was shaped by huge glaciers that once covered the northern part of the continent. As the glaciers melted, lakes, mountains, and rivers were left behind.

Europe has many rivers, including the Rhine, Rhone, and Danube. These waterways form a network that connects people and countries. This continent is also surrounded by bays, fjords, and seas.

There are more than 25,000 **species** of plants and 260 species of **mammals** in Europe. A wide variety of birds can be spotted on the European continent as well. Each **habitat** has plants and animals **adapted** to live there.

Almost 1/2 of the land in Europe is covered in forests.

Europe is home to

85

species of amphibians.

Brown bears are the LARGEST land predators in Europe.

More than 100,000 species of invertebrates can be found in Europe.

The European beaver is the largest rodent on the continent.

The Eurasian brown bear is thought to have migrated to Europe from China. It is now found throughout northern Europe and Asia.

Unique European Life

Europe has a variety of plants, insects, mammals, and birds. Some of these species are native to Europe. Species that are found only in one region are called endemic. Species can be endemic for a couple of reasons. Climate and geography play a key role in forming the habitat needed for specific species. Often, species become endemic to one region because their habitat has been destroyed in other areas.

Europe has many plant and animal species, and certain areas are known for endemic species. More than three quarters of European amphibian species are endemic, as well as half of the reptiles. One fourth of all mammal species in Europe are endemic.

One area known for its endemic species is a rugged landscape on the eastern border of Europe and Asia. The Caucasus region has about 1,600 species of plants that are found only there. Nine of these plant species are found in the area's mountain ranges, where they thrive on the high elevation and cold temperatures. The Caucasian salamander is one of the region's few endemic amphibians, while the Caucasian snowcock is the area's only endemic bird species. The area also has about 20 endemic mammal species and at least 20 endemic reptile species.

Caucasus Region

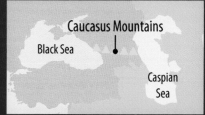

The Caucasus is home to 380 bird species, 130 mammal species, 125 fish species, and 90 species of reptile.

Caspian seals can live to be 50 years old in nature.

Several Caucasian lizard species have no males. The females reproduce on their own.

The venom of the Caucasian viper is used in surgery to stop bleeding.

At 1,740 square miles (4,500 sq. km), the West Caucasian tur has the smallest range of any living ungulate, or hoofed animal.

One quarter of the region's plant species are endemic.

The West Caucasian tur can be found in the Caucasus Mountains, at elevations ranging between 2,625 and 13,780 feet (800 and 4,200 m).

Where in the World?

Europe is located in the northern hemisphere. It lies north of the **equator** and is connected to the Asian continent to the east. The Ural Mountains are generally considered to form Europe's eastern border.

Europe borders two oceans, the Arctic Ocean to the north and Atlantic Ocean to the west. The Mediterranean, Black, and Caspian Seas form the southern border.

The climate of Europe is as varied as the land itself. The parts of Europe that lie closest to the equator have more sunlight and more constant temperatures. These factors affect the kinds of plants and animals that thrive there. Regions north of the equator have greater ranges in temperature. The plants and animals living farther north are adapted to these varied temperatures.

European Biomes

A large area that has a similar climate, terrain, plants, and animals is called a biome. Though similar biomes are found throughout the world, the types of plants and animals living there are usually unique to the continent. Europe has several biomes. Its main land biomes are chaparral, tundra, taiga, mixed forest, and grassland.

Beezley Falls in Great Britain is an ecosystem in the mixed forest biome.

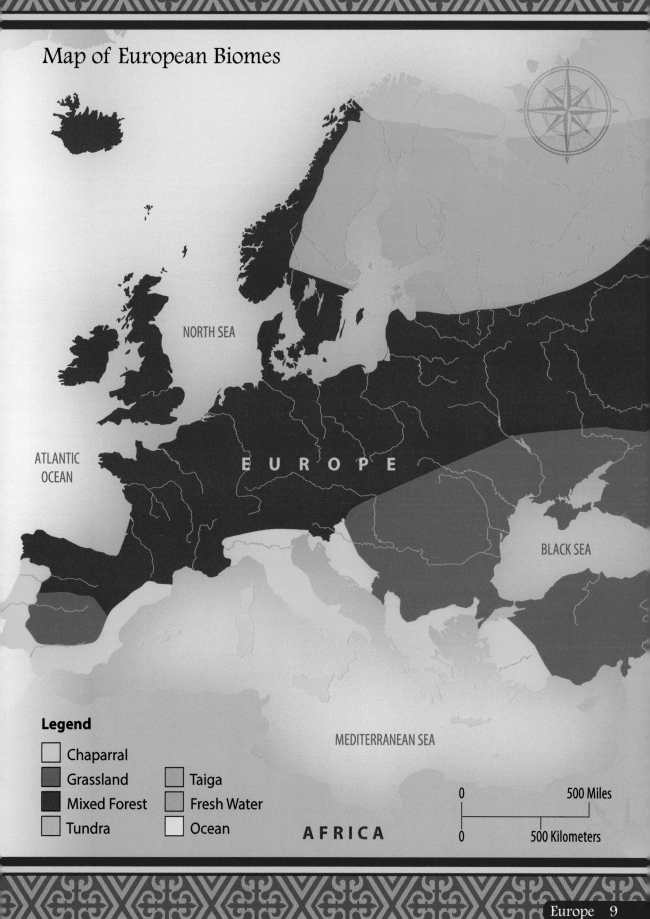

Map of European Biomes

NORTH SEA

ATLANTIC
OCEAN

E U R O P E

BLACK SEA

Legend

☐ Chaparral

☐ Grassland ☐ Taiga

☐ Mixed Forest ☐ Fresh Water

☐ Tundra ☐ Ocean

MEDITERRANEAN SEA

A F R I C A

0   500 Miles

0   500 Kilometers

European Land Biomes

Each European biome has its own characteristics. However, the biomes in Europe all share similar characteristics with the same biomes on other continents. The types of animals and plants found in these biomes also share similar traits.

Tundra

This biome has a very cold and harsh climate. The land is covered in snow much of the year. The ground often remains frozen, so plants only grow for a few months when thawing occurs.

Plants: Only low-growing plants thrive in the tundra because of the high winds and cold temperatures. Other vegetation includes lichens and mosses. No trees grow in this biome.

Animals: Ibexes, polar bears, lemmings, wolverines, and arctic hares are found in the tundra. Several species have thick fur to keep them warm. This fur also acts as **camouflage**.

Winter
Below −30°F
(−35° C)
Summer
35 to 55°F
(2 to 13°C)

Rainfall
Less than **10"**, mostly snow
(25 cm)

Taiga

This biome is located farther south than the tundra. The taiga has long, cold winters, with average temperatures below freezing. The summers are fairly short, and temperatures remain cool.

Plants: Plant life is dominated by large evergreen forests. Many needle-leafed trees grow in the taiga's forests.

Animals: Taiga animals include herbivores such as elk and deer, as well as hares, minks, wolves, and wolverines. Some birds and animals migrate south to avoid the cold winter. Others hibernate or create burrows underground.

Winter
−65 to 20°F
(−54 to 4°C)
Summer
30 to 70°F
(−1 to 21°C)

Rainfall
12 to 33"
(30 to 84 cm)

The exact species that live in a biome are different for each continent and region within the continent. These animal and plant species are adapted to the region's climate and terrain. For example, the tundra biome is home to deer that can live in cold temperatures. However, deer living in the European tundra may be different from deer living in the tundra biome of North America.

Mixed Forest

The mixed forest biome has warm temperatures during summer months and cool temperatures in winter. The change in temperature means that plant and animal life must adapt to a range of conditions.

Plants: Deciduous trees, such as maple and hickory, are found in this biome. Smaller bushes and trees, such as dogwoods, are found here as well. Moss and lichens grow close to the ground.
Animals: The mixed forests attract a variety of animal and bird species. Squirrels, bears, deer, foxes, wolves, and eagles inhabit the forests.

Winter Average −22°F (−30°C)
Summer Average 86°F (30°C)

Rainfall 20 to 60" (51 to 152 cm)

Grassland

The grassland biome of Europe is very dry and experiences warm summers and cold winters. Grass is the dominant feature of the biome. There is little protection from strong winds because very few trees can grow.

Plants: The most abundant types of plants in this biome are different species of grasses. Poor soil quality means that few plants and trees grow there.
Animals: Grassland biomes attract animals that feed on grass, such as deer and bison. **Carnivores** such as foxes and badgers are also found here.

Winter Average −40°F (−40°C)
Summer Average 104°F (40°C)

Rainfall 10 to 30" (25 to 76 cm)

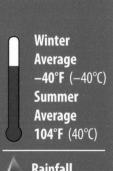

European Ecosystems and Habitats

Every biome is made up of many different ecosystems. Ecosystems are made up of the plants, animals, and other living things that live, feed, and reproduce in the same environment. An ecosystem can be as small as a single tree or as large as a forest. The living things in an ecosystem interact and rely on each other and their environment for food and shelter.

Within every ecosystem is a habitat. A habitat is the place where the plants and animals in an ecosystem live. Habitats supply the needs of these organisms, including food, water, a survivable temperature, and oxygen. The habitat of an insect population may be as small as a plant. The population of a roaming mammal, such as a wolf, may have a habitat that extends across many miles. The ecosystem is all of the living things and their habitats that depend on each other to survive.

The Bialowieza Forest remains much as it was thousands of years ago. It is protected land with strict rules for tourists.

In central Europe, the Bialowieza Forest is one of the best **preserved** forests on the continent. The vast forest features old-growth trees that shelter wolves, brown bears, and European bison.

The Eurasian Steppe runs from the eastern border of Europe into Asia. Here, the dry climate is able to support only short grasses. These grasses attract grazing animals.

The Siberian Tundra has long and cold winters, and the soil is frozen much of the year. Fungi, grasses, and some low shrubs can grow there. Animals living there have extra fat and thick fur. Many birds living in the tundra migrate south for the winter.

Fallow deer are found throughout western Europe. Their spotted coats help camouflage them in the summer.

Plant Life in Europe

Europe's plants have adapted features to suit the conditions of their habitat. The environment of the tundra supports different types of lichens and mosses, which can withstand the harsh conditions. Lichen is also found in the taiga. Large forests of **coniferous** trees also grow here. Mixed forests of coniferous and deciduous trees are found farther south. The deciduous trees are broad-leaved to absorb sunlight. Both coniferous and deciduous forests cover about 30 percent of the continent. The chaparral supports lower-growing species of plants, including small trees and shrubs.

Olive trees are known for their twisted, gnarled trunks.

Olive Tree

The olive tree has been an important part of the Mediterranean region for thousands of years. The fruit is used for oil and is a staple in the diet of the people. The olive tree has thick, leathery leaves and grows small white or yellowish-white flowers. The olive fruit is purple-black and contains a pit in the center.

Norway Spruce

The Norway spruce grows in cool climates, in open areas with plenty of sunlight. This tree has dark green needles and reddish-brown bark. In late spring, the Norway spruce grows cones that are between 4 and 7 inches (10 and 17 cm) in length. They are the largest cones of any spruce tree. The Norway spruce itself grows from 130 to 215 feet (39 to 65 m) tall.

The Norway spruce is native to Europe and was introduced to North America as an ornamental tree.

Adonis Vernalis

Adonis vernalis grows in the steppe region of Europe. The plant, which blooms in early spring, has delicate leaves and a golden flower. This flower is sought after for medicine and is used to treat heart disease. Unfortunately, the flower is very rare and can only be found in the wild. In many countries, it is illegal to pick the plant.

Adonis vernalis is known by several other names, including false hellebore and pheasant's eye.

Lavender

Lavender is originally from Greece, a country in southwest Europe. However, it is now found all over the world. This plant produces small, purple flowers. The leaves of the plant are covered in tiny hairs, which contain essential oils. These oils have been used for thousands of years as medicine and to create perfume, air freshener, and insect repellent.

Prized for their scent, lavender species are now farmed throughout the world.

Just the Facts

Approximately 1/4 of all the world's forests are found in Europe.

The Bialowieza Forest dates back to 8,000 BC.

Woad, a plant of the mustard family, has been used to make blue dye for more than 6,000 years.

The national flower of Malta is the purple-flowered Maltese rock-centaury.

Lavender is from the same plant family as mint, thyme, sage, and rosemary.

Insects, Reptiles, and Amphibians

Beetles, butterflies, bees, and numerous other species of insects are found throughout Europe. New species continue to be discovered. Approximately 20 new insect species were found in central Europe in 2012. Insects are common prey for amphibians and reptiles. Frogs, newts, salamanders, and toads are some of the amphibian species found on the continent. European reptiles include snakes, lizards, and tortoises. Many of Europe's diverse amphibian and reptile species are endemic.

The Italian cave salamander is endemic to the Apennines, a mountain range in central Italy.

Cave Salamander

Cave salamanders are found in central Europe. They live in dark underground caves or on the forest floor. One species has skin that appears white or almost transparent. Males are larger than females and grow to 12 inches (30 cm) long. Some cave salamanders have undeveloped eyes, so they cannot see. They have **gills**, although they use their lungs to breathe.

Spruce Bark Beetle

The **larvae** of the spruce bark beetle grow and feed on the inner bark of trees. Generally, the beetle prefers to feed on thicker-barked trees, such as spruce. Adult beetles grow from 0.17 to 0.22 inches (4.2 to 5.5 mm) in length. The beetle's color varies between red, dark brown, and completely black. Its body is covered with long yellow hairs.

Spruce bark beetles can cause serious damage to spruce forests if the trees become infested.

Moor Frog

The moor frog is a small amphibian native to Europe. The frog is generally reddish brown in color, but some are yellow, gray, or light green, with a white belly. During mating season, the male moor frog will sometimes turn bright blue to attract mates. Moor frogs are 2 to 3 inches (5 to 8 cm) long. Tadpoles eat algae and small invertebrates, while adult moor frogs feed on insects.

Mating season takes place between March and June. The male moor frog is blue for only a couple of days during this time.

Common Adder

As the name suggests, the common adder is a species of snake found throughout Europe. It is a member of the viper family and can be found in different areas, including grassy fields and rocky slopes. The adder's poisonous venom can cause tissue damage to humans. Some common adders are completely black while others have a zigzag pattern along their backs.

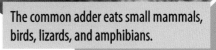

The common adder eats small mammals, birds, lizards, and amphibians.

Just the Facts

Europe has 482 species of butterflies.

One species of giant earthworm, *Lumbricus badensis*, is found only in the Black Forest in central Europe.

Europe is home to 151 species of reptiles.

Only 2 species of tree frogs live in Europe.

A peacock butterfly's wings have two blue spots that look like eyes to frighten predators.

Birds and Mammals

European bird and mammal species have adapted to their different habitats. Many species found in the tundra, such as reindeer, migrate south to avoid the extreme winter conditions. Other mammal species stay in the region and use their thick fur to protect them from the cold. Some animals have adapted to avoid predators. Birds such as white partridges and woodpeckers have coloring that helps them blend in with their woodland homes. Quail, the gray partridge, and other birds found in the European steppes rely on their gray or brown feathers to keep them hidden in the dry grass.

The saker falcon is normally found in steppes and open plains.

Saker Falcon

The saker falcon is a large bird of prey found in southeast Europe. The falcon grows to approximately 18 inches (46 cm) tall, with a very wide wingspan. It feeds on small mammals such as voles, rats, chipmunks, and other birds. In order to catch its prey, the saker falcon dives at speeds up to 200 miles (321.8 km) per hour. Other than humans, the saker falcon has no natural enemies.

Wolverine

Wolverines are a type of weasel that live in the forests of northern Europe. They are ferocious predators and use their powerful jaws to catch and eat their food. Wolverines feed on rodents, birds, fish, and eggs, as well as fruit and plants. A wolverine is typically 26 to 34 inches (66 to 86 cm) in length, and has a 7 to 10 inch (18 to 25 cm) tail. Its average life span is between 4 and 6 years.

The wolverine's thick fur is water-repellent and resistant to frost.

Barbary Macaque

The Barbary macaque is a large species of monkey that has no tail. Its fur can be gray, brown, or yellow. Its face is dark pink. The Barbary macaque has large cheek pouches in which it can store food. It feeds on fruit, leaves, bark, and roots. Males are slightly larger than females and grow from 22 to 28 inches (55 to 71 cm) long.

The island of Gibraltar is the only place Barbary macaques are found on the European continent.

Capercaillie

The capercaillie is commonly known as the wood grouse. It is the largest bird in the grouse family and is about the size of a turkey. The female capercaillie is about half the size of the male. The female's brown coloring helps camouflage it from predators while it roosts on its nest. The male is chocolate brown. It has green coloring along its chest, white on its wings and tail, and red above each eye. Capercaillies often build their nests in hollows under trees. This leaves them vulnerable to predators.

Male capercaillies are best known for the gurgling and tapping sounds they make to attract females.

European Aquatic Biomes

Besides the different land biomes, Europe also has aquatic biomes. The two main types of aquatic biome are freshwater and marine. The difference between these two biomes is the salt content in the water. Marine biomes have a higher concentration of salt.

Aquatic Ecosystems and Habitats

Aquatic biomes consist of different ecosystems and habitats. Fish, seaweed, and aquatic mammals are found in the waters in and around the European continent. The cold water off the North Atlantic coast supports several cold-water coral reefs. Unlike tropical coral reefs, these species of coral can survive with less sunlight. Cold-water corals can grow at greater depths.

Marine Biome

Oceans and coral reefs are part of Europe's marine biome. Oceans are the largest part of the biome.

Marine biomes are subdivided based on the depth from the water's surface. Ocean water closer to the surface receives more sunlight than deeper areas of the ocean. Warmer temperatures and more sunlight allow different types of plants to grow. This attracts animals that differ from those found in deeper, colder, and darker waters.

Plants: Marine algae, kelp, and seaweed grow in Europe's marine biome.

About 3% salt content

Animals: Coral, fish, sea turtles, sharks, whales, and seals live in and around the waters of the marine biome.

The Mediterranean Sea has an area of more than 1,000,000 square miles (2,700,000 sq. km). Water from the Mediterranean Sea flows into the Atlantic Ocean and the Black Sea. By comparison, the Caspian Sea has the largest surface area of any lake in the world. It spans an area of 143,000 square miles (370,000 sq. km). Other large European lakes, such as Lakes Ladoga and Onega in Russia, are home to a variety of freshwater plant and animal life.

Cold-water corals are found at depths between 130 and 6,560 feet (40 and 2,000 m), at temperatures as low as 39°F (4°C).

Freshwater Biome

Europe's freshwater biomes include ponds, lakes, streams, rivers, and wetlands. Each has different characteristics.

Water in lakes and ponds is usually at a constant level and contains a large supply of nutrients. In rivers and streams, flow rates affect the kinds of life that can survive. The water level in wetlands varies depending on the amount of rainfall and the season of the year.

Plants: Algae, reeds, and grasses can be found growing in the freshwater biomes.

Less than 1% salt content

Animals: Europe's freshwater biomes are home to fish, snails, and turtles.

European Aquatic Life

The temperature, nutrients, and oxygen in the water affect the kinds of life that exist in freshwater and marine biomes. The main plant life is algae. Different algae species have adapted to live in either freshwater or saltwater biomes, but not both. Specific fish species are also classified as freshwater and marine varieties. Europe has 546 species of freshwater fish, and approximately 1,100 species of marine fish. Aquatic environments are also home to a variety of bird and mammal species.

The Mediterranean monk seal is one of the most endangered mammals in the world. It is estimated that only about 600 exist.

Monk Seal

The monk seal lives in the waters of the Mediterranean Sea. It has a brown or gray coat, which becomes pale underwater. Male monk seals are known for the distinct white patch on their bellies. As males age, their coats become darker in color, but the white patch remains. The male monk seal weighs about 695 pounds (315 kg). The female is slightly smaller, weighing about 660 pounds (300 kg).

Gizani

The gizani is a small freshwater fish that is endemic to Greece. It has a silver body with a dark stripe that runs along each side. This fish has no teeth, but has bones in its throat to chew its food. The gizani eats small aquatic insects and their larvae, along with some plants.

In nature, the gizani has a life span of only three years.

Neptune Grass

Neptune grass is a flowering marine plant found only in the Mediterranean Sea. The grass creates large, thick meadows along the sea floor. These meadows provide shelter for many marine animals, making the grass an important part of the ecosystem. Neptune grass is tall and grows slowly but lives for a long time. The grass is able to resist changes in the environment, which has helped it to survive.

Fibers from the leaves of Neptune grass sometimes form balls that wash up on shorelines.

European Otter

The European otter lives in freshwater areas throughout the European continent. Its long body is covered in thick brown fur. The otters can grow from 22 to 28 inches (56 to 71 cm) in length. They have strong, thick tails and webbed paws, which help them to swim and catch fish. The European otter is hunted by wolves, lynx, and large birds of prey.

The European otter can also be found in Asia and northern Africa.

Just the Facts

Only 2 species of sea turtles, the loggerhead and the green, make their nests in the Mediterranean Sea.

16% of European aquatic plant species are endemic.

Pelicans and flamingos are found in the delta of the Volga River in Russia.

Some of Europe's cold-water coral is **8,500** years old.

Europe is home to 41 species of marine mammals.

Maintaining Balance

The variety of plant and animal life is an essential part of the European environment. Every ecosystem depends on a complex balance of interactions between the living things in that ecosystem. Temperature and rainfall affect the types of plants that can survive in an area. These plants supply food and shelter to insects, amphibians, reptiles, birds, and mammals. Any change in an ecosystem can affect the living things in that environment. These effects can be both positive and negative.

Introducing New Species

It is estimated that more than 10,000 species of plants and animals have been introduced to the European continent. Many of these plants have had a positive impact on the continent and the people who live there. Plants such as rice, sugarcane, oats, and corn are now grown as an important food source. In other cases, however, introducing new species can have a negative effect on the environment.

American skunk cabbage was introduced in Europe as an ornamental plant. It has since begun to grow in nature, where it overshadows smaller native plants. Unable to receive sunlight, most of these native species disappear within a few years.

The native species in an ecosystem have adapted over many generations to survive in that environment. When a foreign species is introduced, it may have no natural predators. The population of the new species continues to increase because there is no interaction to keep it in balance. When allowed to grow freely, these species take over land that was home to the native species. The native species are forced to live in smaller areas. Over time, they can face extinction. It is estimated that approximately 10 to 15 percent of non-native species in Europe have had a negative impact on the European environment.

Ecosystem Interactions

All living things within an ecosystem interact with each other. A food chain diagrams the interaction among producers, consumers, and decomposers. Producers are plants that use the Sun's energy to make food. Primary consumers are herbivores that eat the plants. Secondary consumers feed on herbivores. Decomposers break down dead organisms and return nutrients to the soil.

Norway Spruce
Norway spruce trees are producers. They provide food and shelter for red squirrels.

Red Squirrel
Red squirrels are primary consumers. They live in Norway spruce trees and feed on fungi and the seeds from the tree. They often spread the tree's seeds by burying them in the ground and leaving them there.

Great Gray Owl
Great gray owls are secondary consumers. They prey on red squirrels and will sometimes rest in a tree such as the Norway spruce.

Spruce Bark Beetle
Spruce bark beetles burrow into the bark of the Norway spruce to lay their eggs. The eggs feed on the bark of the tree.

Fungi
Fungi are decomposers. They break down dead plant matter for nutrients. Fungi provide food for red squirrels.

Diversity for Humans

People around the world rely on Europe's plants and animals for food. Europe is a major exporter of crops such as rice, corn, wheat, and potatoes. To preserve the health of these crops, it is important that there is **diversity** within each plant species. If plants are too similar, they will be vulnerable to the same diseases and pests. Entire crops can be eliminated as a result.

To avoid this situation, European scientists have been using wild relatives of certain plants to strengthen the farm crops. By introducing **genes** from the wild relatives into the farm crops, scientists have been able to improve the nutritional content of the crops and produce crops that are more resistant to pests and disease. This allows for healthier and more abundant crops.

Over time, land development has impacted Europe's biodiversity. Today, approximately 43 percent of land in the Europe is used for agricultural purposes.

Human Impact

Humans have been shaping the European environment for hundreds of years. Europe's small land area and large population leave little room for natural habitats. Land has been cleared for agriculture and to build towns and cities. Clearing land is a major threat to native habitats and the species that rely on those habitats for food and shelter. Populations of birds, insects, butterflies, and amphibians have declined in the last 30 years. Rivers and lakes have been changed by the construction of dams, overfishing, and pollution. These changes affect the living things that rely on aquatic habitats.

Scientists perform studies and experiments on plants in greenhouses and other facilities to determine how to improve the health of food crops.

Conserving Nature

In an effort to **conserve** the diverse ecosystems of Europe, several countries have set up nature reserves. These reserves are protected lands that cannot be developed. They conserve habitats for the plant and animal species that live there. The Coto Doñana National Park in Spain contains breeding pairs for about half of all native European bird species. Gran Paradiso National Park, in the Alps near Turin, Italy, has helped preserve the habitat of the Alpine ibex, which was close to extinction. Governments, local and international organizations, and individuals are helping to protect European species. They do this by raising public awareness and promoting positive use of resources.

Coto Doñana National Park is the summer home for more than 500,00 birds. Bewick's swans spend the summer in the tundra and move to the temperate regions during winter.

Make an Ecosystem Web

Use this book and research on the Internet to create a European ecosystem.

1. Find a European plant or animal. Think about what habitat it lives in.
2. Find at least three organisms that are found in the same habitat. This could include plants, insects, amphibians, reptiles, birds, and mammals.
3. How do these species interact with each other? Do they provide food or shelter for the other organisms?
4. Begin linking these organisms together to show which organisms rely on each other for food or shelter.
5. Once your ecosystem web is complete, think about how removing one organism would affect the other organisms in the web.

European Ecosystem

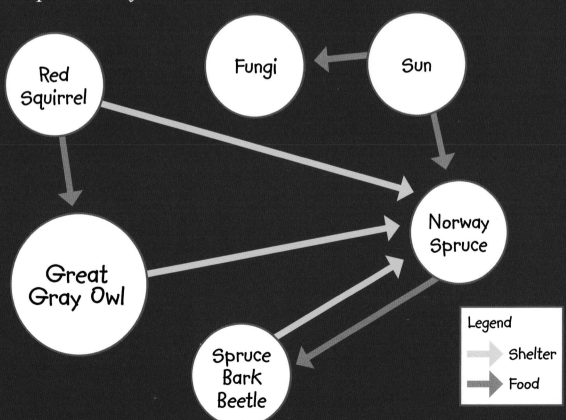

Quiz

1 What other continent is attached to Europe?

Asia

2 How many species of endemic plants are found in the Caucasus?

About 1,600

3 What are the four major biomes found in Europe?

Mixed forest, grassland, taiga, and tundra

6 What features do animals in the tundra have for protection from cold temperatures?

Extra fat and thick fur

4 Which biome is found in the most northerly parts of Europe?

Tundra

9 Which aquatic biome has the most salt water?

The marine biome

7 Which species of spruce tree grows the largest cones?

Norway spruce

5 What four needs does a habitat supply for an organism?

Food, water, temperature, and oxygen

8 What does the male moor frog do to attract mates?

It turns a bright blue

10 What are two reasons land is cleared in Europe?

For agriculture and to build towns and cities

Key Words

adapted: changed to suit the environment

camouflage: to hide or disguise by blending into the surroundings

carnivores: meat-eating animals

coniferous: trees or shrubs that grow cones and have evergreen leaves

conserve: protect something from destruction

deciduous: tree or shrub that loses its leaves every year

diversity: having a great amount of variety and differences

equator: an imaginary horizontal line that marks the center of the Earth

genes: tiny units in a cell that determine the features an offspring inherits from its parents

gills: organs that underwater animals use to breathe

habitat: the area or region where an organism lives

larvae: a newly-hatched insect

mammals: animals that have hair or fur and give birth to live young

preserved: kept in its original state

species: a group of animals capable of breeding and producing young

Index

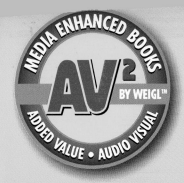

Log on to www.av2books.com

AV² by Weigl brings you media enhanced books that support active learning. Go to www.av2books.com, and enter the special code found on page 2 of this book. You will gain access to enriched and enhanced content that supplements and complements this book. Content includes video, audio, weblinks, quizzes, a slide show, and activities.

AV² Online Navigation

Book Pages
AV² pages directly correspond to pages in the book.

Audio
Listen to sections of the book read aloud.

Video
Watch informative video clips.

Key Words
Study vocabulary, and complete a matching word activity.

Quizzes
Test your knowledge.

Slide Show
View images and captions, and prepare a presentation.

Embedded Weblinks
Gain additional information for research.

Try This!
Complete activities and hands-on experiments.

AV² was built to bridge the gap between print and digital. We encourage you to tell us what you like and what you want to see in the future.

Sign up to be an AV² Ambassador at www.av2books.com/ambassador.